Kristi Yamaguchi

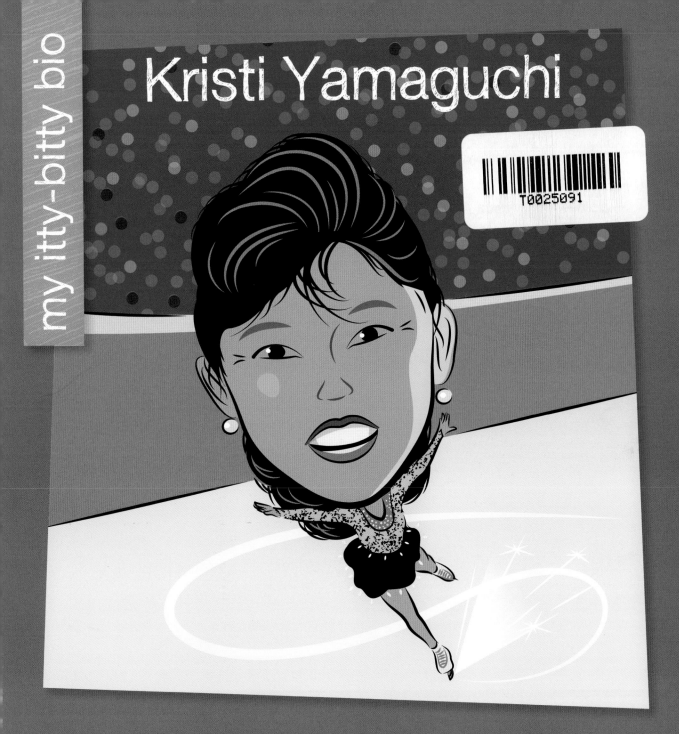

CHERRY LAKE PRESS

Published in the United States of America by Cherry Lake Publishing Group
Ann Arbor, Michigan
www.cherrylakepublishing.com

Reading Adviser: Beth Walker Gambro, MS, Ed., Reading Consultant, Yorkville, IL
Book Designer: Jennifer Wahi
Illustrator: Jeff Bane

Photo Credits: page 5: © Sundry Photography/Shutterstock; page 7: © Maria Sbytova/Shutterstock; pages 9, 22: © Prostock-studio/Shutterstock; pages 11, 15, 23: © PCN Photography/Alamy Stock Photo; page 13: © sportpoint/Shutterstock; page 17: © Kimimasa Mayama KM/CRB/REUTERS/Alamy Stock Photo; page 19: © Ray Stubblebine RFS/REUTERS/Alamy Stock Photo; page 21: © Carrienelson1/Dreamstime.com

Cherry Lake Press is an imprint of Cherry Lake Publishing Group.

Library of Congress Cataloging-in-Publication Data

Names: Loh-Hagan, Virginia, author. | Bane, Jeff, illustrator.
Title: Kristi Yamaguchi / by Virginia Loh-Hagan ; illustrated by Jeff Bane.

Description: Ann Arbor, Michigan : Cherry Lake Publishing, 2023. | Series: My itty-bitty bio | Audience: Grades K-1 | Summary: "This biography for early readers examines the life of former figure skater and Olympic gold medalist Kristi Yamaguchi in a simple, age-appropriate way that helps young readers develop word recognition and reading skills. Includes table of contents, author biography, timeline, glossary, index, and other informative backmatter. The My Itty-Bitty Bio series celebrates diversity, covering women and men from a range of backgrounds and professions including immigrants and individuals with disabilities"-- Provided by publisher.
Identifiers: LCCN 2022042689 | ISBN 9781668920169 (paperback) | ISBN 9781668919149 (hardcover) | ISBN 9781668922828 (pdf) | ISBN 9781668921494 (ebook)
Subjects: LCSH: Yamaguchi, Kristi--Juvenile literature. | Figure skaters--United States--Biography--Juvenile literature. | Women figure skaters--United States--Biography--Juvenile literature.
Classification: LCC GV850.Y36 L65 2023 | DDC 796.91/2/092 [B]--dc23/eng/20220909
LC record available at https://lccn.loc.gov/2022042689

Printed in the United States of America
Corporate Graphics

About the author: When not writing, Dr. Virginia Loh-Hagan serves as the Director of the Asian Pacific Islander Desi American (APIDA) Center at San Diego State University. She identifies as Chinese American and is committed to amplifying APIDA communities. She lives in San Diego with her very tall husband and very naughty dogs.

About the illustrator: Jeff Bane and his two business partners own a studio along the American River in Folsom, California, home of the 1849 Gold Rush. When Jeff's not sketching or illustrating for clients, he's either swimming or kayaking in the river to relax.

my story

I was born in 1971 in California. I am Japanese American. I grew up with a brother and sister.

I was born with **club feet**. My feet were crooked. They were weak. I had to wear a cast for the first few years.

I took skating lessons. Skating made my feet stronger. I also learned **ballet**. My legs got stronger.

What dances do you like?

I loved ice skating. I started **competing**. I did well. I was very shy. But I did not feel shy when I skated.

I was graceful on the ice. I did jumps. I did spins. I felt free.

13

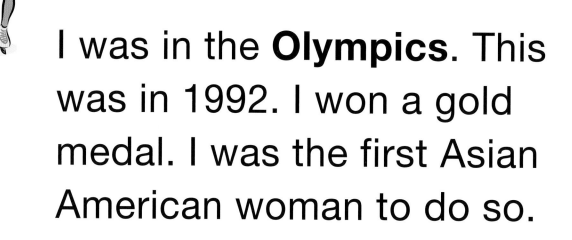

I was in the **Olympics**. This was in 1992. I won a gold medal. I was the first Asian American woman to do so.

What is your favorite Olympic sport to watch?

I became a **professional** skater.
I toured. I was on TV.

I designed clothes. I wrote books. I served the community. I got married. We have two children.

I am a champion. I am a famous ice skater. I am a mother. I inspire others.

What would you like to ask me?

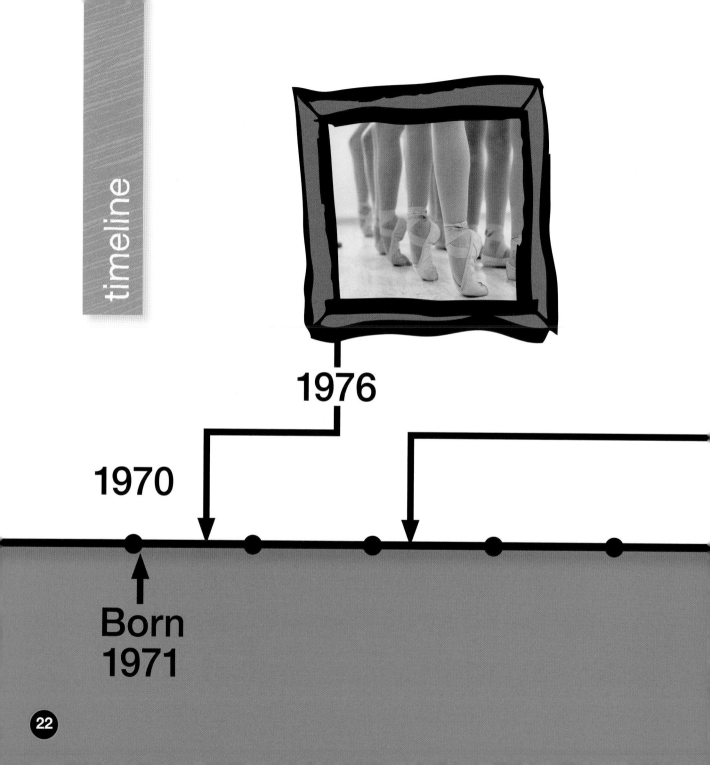

1976

1970

Born
1971

1992

2070

glossary & index

glossary

ballet (BAH-lay) a classical dance form demanding grace and flowing movements

club feet (KLUHB FEET) a birth defect in which feet are twisted out of shape

competing (kuhm-PEE-ting) striving to outdo another person in a contest for a prize

Olympics (uh-LIM-piks) international sports competitions

professional (pruh-FEH-shuh-nuhl) earning a living in a sport or other job

index